THAT'S WHERE YOU COME IN

CMUP Poetry
Jake Grefenstette, Series Editor

Books by John Skoyles

POETRY

A Little Faith
Permanent Change
Definition of the Soul
The Situation
Suddenly It's Evening: Selected Poems
Inside Job
Yes and No

PROSE

Generous Strangers
Secret Frequencies: A New York Education
A Moveable Famine: A Life in Poetry
The Nut File
Driven
All the Question Marks

THAT'S WHERE YOU COME IN

John Skoyles

Carnegie Mellon University Press
Pittsburgh 2026

Acknowledgments

Grateful acknowledgment is given to the editors of the journals in which the following poems first appeared:

American Imago: "Elegy for My Father"
Commonweal: "Poem for a Summer Morning" and "Token Entry"
Jung Journal: Culture and Psyche: "The Hospital Angel"
The Nation: "The Beginning"
On the Seawall: "At the Golden Cue," "Silk Bouquet," and "Roback"
Plume: "Bill Knott," "Three Wishes," "Personal," "Sheila-Who-Sees," "Her Pencils," "A Drink with My Late Uncle," "That's Where You Come In," "Can't Explain," "Calvary Cemetery," "Return Home," and "Unrequited"
The Poetry Review: "Goodbye and Hello"

And many thanks to Jonathan Aaron for his invaluable editorial eye and friendship.

Cover art: Diana Horowitz, *South from Uptown #1*, 2022, oil on canvasboard, 6 x 6 inches. Image courtesy of the artist and Bookstein Projects, New York.

Book design by Connie Amoroso

Library of Congress Control Number 2026937112
ISBN 978-0-88748-743-9

Printed and bound in the United States of America

10 9 8 7 6 5 4 3 2 1

for Betsy Aidem

After the final no there comes a yes
And on that yes the future world depends.

—Wallace Stevens

Contents

I

II

III

I

Aspects of a Snowstorm

No words today
only footfalls

along this path,
a sentence

you follow
to its end,

sounds without syllables.
A blank book

because here
you write your own

as you walk
asking directions

of the sun
which answers

from a tall threshold
some call the heavens,

allowing you
to negate,

for a moment,
your self-destructive

brand of fate
and believe

or not,
as is the case.

Nunc

On Christmas Eve, I circled the chapel,
one of the choir boys singing and tilting
candles toward our palms to gather wax.

Holy water scooped from the font
drenched the soloist's skin
when his surplice caught fire.

After Mass, the tenors took us to Finn's
for underage bottles of Bud.

My mother insisted I bring my wool hat.

She knew we'd be marching
home in the snow, caroling Latin.

My favorite word was *nunc*,
meaning *now*, but that was then.

Back Then

Everyone was either a cop, a crook, a victim or a snitch.

We saw stop signs as obstacles
to the free will of street life
and clanged them in passing with our open palms.

Guilty of something, innocent of almost everything,
we lacked the imagination
to know what we missed.

Music we never heard, the fugues of Bach
for instance, was stronger than silence.

Never alone, we hated being home—
my father drank spilled coffee from the saucer
as if that liquid saved his life.
He'd sipped at the trough of mirages for so long.

There was no boat to take us away,
just a raft of ice cream sticks floating down
the gutter's stream with a gum wrapper for a sail.

We followed it to the sewer,
and some of us jumped in.

Mourning Dove

There's no room on the schoolhouse sill,
so this dove stalks the sidewalk ice.
Little remains of his ritual
for rival or mate, just the wind
that clips his wings to fluff.
His eyes squint shut. He can't lift off
the concrete square to compete
in open air's game of *Too Late, Time's Up.*
Neither you nor I will see him
vanish between this life and the next.

Two Men

When the front wheel of a thick and rusty Schwinn
pushed its way into Cousin's Pub,
we could have guessed it was Francis Silva, Iron Man,
banned from every bar in town.

Francis leaned his bike against the wall,
its steel reminding us
that his nickname came from bending
the frame of a jail cell door.

The room's quiet was broken
by a barking dog outside
that stirred the dog
at the feet of Howling Jack, himself asleep.

The bartender asked Francis to leave,
but he kept pacing back and forth
as if in a shoe store and feeling for the fit.

He made no sound but kept his eyes on
the glass skyline of shapes and strengths
from which so many of us leapt
without leaving the ground.

When no one offered to buy him a beer—
it wasn't allowed—
Francis raised and dropped his bike hard
and swore he'd send us to our graves.

"What do I have to lose," he said, bowing his head.

Our bartender displayed his phone,
threatening to make a call.

Francis Silva, Iron Man, like each of us
two men in one, found what he'd been looking for
and found it out of reach.

We continued drinking,
as we did before he crossed the threshold
of just one more.

He turned and rolled his bike back toward the door.

A Drink with My Late Uncle

A detail like a grave
won't stand in the way

of his shaking my hand
on the patio of his rooftop garden.

He was the first to tap
my hidden self on the shoulder

and open our menu of shared traits.
Scotch for him, sangria

for his underage nephew,
a Macanudo from his suitcoat pocket

providing the ash
out of which he rises today,

reminding me how I trailed him
at sundown to the pagan altars

of cathedral-like bistros.
He walked the zigzag walk

all drunkards walk,
seeing death as nothing

but the aftertaste
of smoldering addictions.

He flicks his stub at a lilac
where it miraculously lands on a leaf.

And when I admire this oddity of balance,
my dropped pencil rests upright

on the eraser end. These headstands
of nature provide an apt setting

for the two of us,
predetermined windup toys

waiting for a child to step on them.
And that child is the god

who made all things. And made all things to pass.
This visit to my wayward uncle ends

when his widow opens the slider,
saying she's swept her hearth's display

of childhood dolls, and lost
Pinocchio's screw-in nose.

The whole point's the nose, she says,
and asks him to look for it later.

He says he will but he's lying.
He'll be here with me. He'll always be with me.

Ancestry

I see him on Broadway, a bulldog with bright eyes
who adores the world, shifting weight,
panting, ready to startle you with his face.
His forebears hung by their teeth from a rope
over a rafter to strengthen their jaws
yet retained the tenderness of a breeze.
He smooched a toddler's cheek near the steps
of St. Pat's on Easter, that day with its baskets
of shredded green plastic, gaudy eggs,
and blossoms from the flowering cherry
my grandmother loved in our yard in Queens.
She left Parma as a teen for New York
and used to say she missed the mountain air
that gave everyone an appetite,
but when they went to the kitchen,
there was nothing to eat. I'm remembering this
at the counter of City Diner.
The guy beside me opens the paper to a full-page ad
for hospice care and says, "My dad's in there."
A goateed man at a nearby booth chokes out
a cough that sounds beyond illness.
He loosens his ascot and leans against the wall
to make himself invisible.
                                        Here we are,
incarnate but absent, fending off dismay,
looking for meaning in clouds, praying
to St. Synchronicity, observing ten commandments,
twelve steps, scratching the numbers.

My mother in her fumbling years looked through
the mesh of a summer screen and praised
the skill that made those million little windows.
Then embraced her son for reporting what he saw
using just twenty-six letters of our alphabet.
It's amazing, she said. *I'm so proud of you.*

Token Entry

Through the turnstile,
uptown or down,

past the bench
where life

sleeps
on its rack

of layers and litter.
The platform's edge

and its oncoming
promise.

We are admitted—
the sick,

the pre,
the post,

the free of suffering
and disease—

deciphering
staticky

apostrophes
from above—

then out
the revolving gate

of before,
after

and beyond.

Calvary Cemetery

My father conducted his burial from the grave.

A loudspeaker near the casket
divided mourners into those who loved
and those who suffered
his favorite semiclassical cassette.

Fistfuls of soil. Wreathes and rain.
The lingering score made it seem
every chord was strummed by a one-man band.

The crowd dispersed into clans,
clans into couples, couples into palm readers
scanning their own hands.

My bloodline led me to the trestle
of my childhood
where my father once placed a penny
on the track, teasing me it would derail the train.

The approaching engine held the freight
of the past, the rush of the present,
and my daydream to dare the future.

The train sped south, the tiny coin crushed
flat, a charm on those tracks
that returned without leaving, left without looking back.

Currency

In this country, our currency is the dream.
When I understood that,

I knew Citibank would take as collateral
my word

that the cottage on the bay
was a dream come true.

To celebrate, I brought my parents
to Bradley's tiny bar which sat just four.

My mother sang, "Whoever named it, named it well.
A bar to heaven and a door to hell"

in that high-pitched tone she always used
to call our dogs to dinner.

When the bartender said
"There is no greater sign of love than . . ."

and "It is one of the beauties of life that . . ."
my father tipped him with the promise

of a dream job at Mayflower Moving.
In the American dream of owning a home,

a trophy wife waits—
my mother had seen her and said she was a doll.

Her name was Donna, but I heard Dollar.
In this country, our currency is the dream.

Columbus Avenue

A little boy cries as if his world will end,
but this taco, bagel, egg roll block
will outlast trends, though a boy
who holds a hand and cries
won't understand the universe
survives despite our tears.
Today he feels just the woe
that comes from longing for a toy
or dog, lost pen, missed fun.
His mother and anyone who hears
never knows how deep or far it goes
or where it ends. It could make him
an understanding friend, or turn his noise
to notes and chords that blend in great halls,
or he might remain a boy who cries
one afternoon, comfort coming late or not at all.

Can’t Explain

Valentine’s Day

I can’t imagine why the phrase
I can’t explain

came to me today,
a day the world swoons

over two people
entering one bedroom.

I can’t explain it,
can you? The Who

sang “I Can’t Explain.”
I can’t imagine how

I forgot that
refrain until today.

It’s a god, imagination,
a god who gives

directions if you ask.
And should you ask,

you’ll arrive
in a Valentine-laden town

where hearts festoon
both sleeves and cards.

Where you call me yours,
I call you mine,

and god calls us
a cab

to a library
where all the anthologies

crash down
with the sound of a train

off the tracks.
And as they collapse

to the floor
of the stacks,

they open to poems
where lovers meet

in rooms reserved
for them alone.

How you and I
got into one of them

I can't explain.

Smidgen

I try to understand
the brotherhood of man,
the Sisters of Mercy,
and why the face
in the photo
on the cabdriver's dash
looks like my ex.
I compare the wrong change
to a high crime, larceny
to a missing slice of lime,
and the parrot's sneeze
to a draft coming down
the hall, without even
a smidgen of understanding
the equations that pretend
one life, one pulse, one breath
is like another, that one death
equals any other life come to an end.

Poem for a Summer Morning

The spider plant and Christmas cactus
don't quite rejoice, yet there's an awakening
at the windows and walls from the rustle
of the garbage truck and overheard phone calls.
We who are left in the city don't care
for the sea or shore at this time of day,
just let us play in the stray ups and downs
because someone has to be around to keep
the sweaty city surviving the news.
We've got nothing to lose except our losses
which subtract from the sum of voices,
faces, sirens, and that glum cat on his sill
asking a question all cats ask which no one's
answered yet except to say it's another day.

Witness and Truth

Last week our waiter called himself
Witness. Last night he said he was Truth.

He poured wine with reverence
and a mortician's touch,

keeping us climbing
after we reached the top of the mountain.

A woman at the bar walked out
and left her face in the mirror.

Every dollar contained the means to get you
blind as a worm, and everyone danced

on a spectacular floor where golden
strobe lights animated dust.

A ponytail caught fire at a table
in the alcove, and the flames were doused

by Witness, or was it Truth?

Between Us

Around us, a park,
and in this park, a bench.

And around this bench, sparrows.
On these sparrows, wings.

And on those wings, feathers.
Under those feathers,

a sparrow
who lost a feather

I waved under your chin
to make you laugh,

and since then there has only been
laughter between us.

The Envelope Salesman

How many orders for watermarked bond
and glassine envelopes did my father write

with this ballpoint pen? Buffing the sheen
on its well-worn barrel summons his ghost

to the downtown block where we used to meet
at day's end, a shift he'd finish

with a click above a ledger—
a feat with which I can't compete.

My job's between me and a blank sheet—
no deciphering the psyche of the buyer at the bank,

or swooping low on marrow bones
to greet the boss good day.

The pen glides, it doesn't furrow,
though I hope it might go deep enough

to recall my father at his office window
tapping a smudged knuckle

toward the awning of a diner
where I wait for the paper and envelope salesman

linked to me through blood and ink.

Compass

I can't read a map,
but I'm never lost

getting to your place.
The car drives itself;

the road finds a way.
The train steams on

overseen by a conductor,
the unlikely cupid

who makes sure
I get off

at your stop,
that space between us

we keep trying
to dissolve.

II

The Beginning

There is no one without his hour,
and the hour for us arrived at dusk
when two sparrows

outside the café pecked crumbs
off the curb, suddenly turning
into birds of great plumage,

both of them singing,
male and female,
unheard of, yet heard

by us at a table
in a Broadway shed
until the dinner hour came to a close,

that hour in the first line
you've already forgotten
because I distracted you

with the conversion of the birds
and the magical crumbs
like words you follow

down the page
until you come to the end
and find yourself facing me.

I tell you I'm starting to fall . . .
but you interrupt, saying *Oh*
and this is the next to last line

and just the beginning.

That's Where You Come In

Captain Jack's Wharf was once alive
with dancing, diving, and the end
of the packed night nowhere in sight.
Then the years came in.

Fall arrived, and the scarf
in the drawer recalled my friend
bringing his cashmere gift to the door.
That's where his ghost came in.

As I drove I-95 closing one eye,
she turned "Twist and Crawl"
way up high. An enabling wife
and the English Beat came in.

She had a bluefish on the line,
but the bent lure brought
just the head to shore.
That's where the seal came in.

The Mighty Quinn came in.
Not the Eskimo from Dylan's song,
but the policeman husband of Katherine Quinn.
And that's where the fist to my chin came in.

When a thunderstorm blacked out our house,
we set candles by the mirror
to double the light,
and that's why the shadows that stayed came in.

Jill came in after my wreck on Route 8,
calming my nerves
on a zebra skin rug
spread before her fireplace.

    The den soon felt
    like a smoldering tomb.
    That's where the blocked flue
    and the fire escape came in.

The therapist said,
"Don't let experience keep you from magic,"
and suddenly disappeared.
That's where a wisp of smoke came in.

    The author of *Shadows of a Larger Hand*
    recommended a twelve-step plan
    where I took a seat between black and blue,
    and that's where the Higher Power came in.

Keith came in with a pint of gin.
He doubted I'd been sober ten years
and asked everyone in the room if it were true.
And that's where you come in.

News

On the deck of the hotel,
we heard a song in the forsythia.

Not the chickadee's familiar *fee-bee*,
nor the warbler's lilt,

but the first four notes
of "New York, New York."

Across our table
and into summer air—

Start spreading the—
we put down the paper.

There was no news.
There were no headlines.

You became invisible
to everyone but me,

and me to you,
over two cups of tea

and a bird missing a note
hiding a word we both knew.

It was the news
about us, and it was true.

Goodbye and Hello

I'll always turn around
after we say goodbye
on one corner or another,
like the leaf that lands
face-up near the oak,
or the raindrop
that salutes the cloud
from its place
in the lake,
like the simile
that slakes its thirst
for truth
by insisting one thing
is like another.
Goodbye is like hello
when you look back at me.

Unrequited

I wanted sprightly Bree to marry me,
twirling and spiraling from street to street,

oasis, mirage, eclipse of my desire.
Laughing Bree in love with spice,

surf, the sky, and sun. The sound of *s*,
but never *Yes.* My sexton and my bishop,

proffering a ring then pulling back
in favor of a swing in the clarifying park.

A step ahead of me on Broadway,
a slinky sphinx to hold but never have.

A sylph who lies in bed but doesn't sleep,
a white noise machine wound in a sheet.

Rouge blesses her cheeks with a rush
as if revived on a roller rink.

Evidential Bree has dusted herself
for fingerprints and found me guilty

though I'd sandpapered the whorls
away from my thoughts of her each day.

Bree's shadow follows mine—
half-Venus, half-feline,

a savage defender
keeping me from the porch

I built for us
with a welcome mat at the door.

My Rival

He has the Tudor house,
a stately car,

travels far on skis,
horseback, and wings,

but never on a prayer,
which is all

I offer here,
hoping you might consider

shifting gears and come
along with me—

we'll spend before we save,
leap before we see

what's over the edge
and make up the same bed.

May I share my life savings
of thousands of pages

worth nothing and everything?
Can I trust you

not to scoff at this sheaf
which makes grief

with my name in it.
An evening star crashed

right through the plate glass
of the living room where

I loved Sheila
and Sheila loved the moon.

Why No Meow

Your father saw God in the cat. No further
discussion. That was that.

Your mother heard Him in the meow.
She believed in *I don't care*

and *I don't care how.*
It's impossible to hold a cat

to account. The meow
comes from so far back

with the force of a vow.
Your sister's kitten hissed

when she gave it a kiss.
She railed at the clouds,

"Why no meow?"
One of life's joys

is to hear that sound.
The men on your block weren't men

who bowed to man or beast,
but with old age

came first and last meows.
Even when a cat's asleep,

it's awake somewhere else,
inside of you,

waiting to be let out.

End of Summer

When the waiter dropped a tray
of martinis, spilled tea
on the next table,
knocked over a lit candle,

and brought the wrong check,
we laughed with the pleasure
of simply being together.
On the way home, we saw

a plane cross the moon
above a pier of dancers
who kept diving into the bay.
You said about the end

of summer, that no one
walks away younger.
The ebbing tide widened
the shoreline, allowing us

to leave the boardwalk
and pass a parade of starfish,
shells, and seaweed tangled
in skate eggs. We walked until

the sun came up and I placed
a period on the sentence
that said when I met you,
the past came to an end.

Conditions

It's a cold Saturday, and I'm playing
the same song I used to play

before being told my apology
has a condition of reciprocity.

Harder conditions exist
on the street below

at the clinic
where visitors and patients

breathe into each other
their mutual love

of life.
Shadows across the building

from this sunny
place on the top floor

agree the day is darker
than before I said I was sorry.

So I keep playing
"You think you know me,

but you will never know me,"
and I thank Louis Moholo

unconditionally for his song
who has no choice but to accept.

Her Pencils

Here are the pencils
she favored:

mechanical, disposable,
and bought by the case

to hover above
student stories

among cups, plates,
and traces of grease

on the kitchen's
glass topped table,

her ephemeral scrawl
to be read

by sleep-deprived
hopefuls.

How much lead
is left

in this one
whose grooved tip

I twist
to find it writes

of her writing
and her life

in this place,
both erased.

My Ex's Birthday Party

I've brought a board game gift
where players move by throwing dice.

We take turns until the take-out
cake arrives, then dim the lights.

The match seems to crouch before it strikes.

Our faces in the window
reflect our private lives,
stripped of their masked and public guise.

Like the candle flame that knows
what's next,
I worry when her lips approach.

She draws a breath with those closed eyes
I now see through,

and wonder what she wishes for
and if it comes true.

Danzig

He chases his tail, circling the same circle,
something he's learned from watching you
cross errands off your list.

If you challenge him to a staring contest,
he'll win by making you laugh.

He cries to go out, and he cries to come in.
You both strain on a leash, but yours is invisible.

Admit sometimes you'd like to change places
with this yellow Lab,
flop into a bed of thyme and speak without an alphabet.

Even when he's asleep, there seems to be something
on his mind—perhaps his idea of an afterlife—
riding in the back of a truck,

or meeting up at Cafe Luxembourg
where he'll order for you,
as you've done for him so many nights,
and pick up the tab.

Later he'll put you in a cab, directing the driver
back to Jackson Heights
and those streets you walked together,
where the real and the imaginary meet.

That Summer

It was the summer of Wim Mertens' music,
pretty Iris Batista, the Delta Dolcevita
fountain pen with mocha ink, and Zero,
the sick runt of a premature litter.
I'd picked up the pen and failed
to describe the nonsense syllables
of bleating Wim and Iris's straight
red hair, but I found the way
after escorting my pet to her death
at the vet's and came home facing
a blank page, saying, "I miss that little dog!"
What place in my life did she fill
that Iris and Mertens left hollow?
Zero loved looking in the cat bed
for the cat, in the kitchen for a crumb,
and in the next yard for the toddler
whose giggles she adored.
I've become an old man, not suddenly,
though it feels like it happened fast
when I recall that summer—
the child now off to war, the dog risen
from the grave to a page on this porch
where I'm reading for the hundredth time
the goodbye letter Iris slipped under the door.

III

Three Wishes

A frog along the clamshell path
provides three wishes and a rash.

Fall from a great height or never fall.

On the palm of my outstretched hand,
a kind of welcome, male to man.

Fall from a great height or not at all.

I dreamt I proposed in a hurricane
and knelt for a marriage that never came.

Fall from a great height or never fall.

The frog must be Sigmund's son,
he counts that dream as number one.

Fall from a great height or not at all.

We settled in for our nightly fix
of cartoon buffoons in politics;

WBGO
from the radio

on the sill,
and a puppy drained of its free will.

Fall from a great height or never fall.

I wanted you to take my name.
My frog friend says he's not to blame

for claiming that as number two.
I make a list of my lives with you,

and remember most the lightning kiss
we risked

by hugging on the beach in rain
as Frankie Dash sang "You've Changed."

Fall from a great height or not at all.

Your face in summer on a pillow,
a candle and its flicker signal

the feverish
fulfillment of a final wish.

Fall from a great height or never fall.

The Hospital Angel

Blood whispering with bone
is the only sound in the room,

and my only visitor's the angel
who just climbed through the window.

From the look of his wings, the long flight
has left him withering and chilled.

If he were human, he'd be dead,
but there's no end

to his ending, no start to his finish.
"Can immortality be taught?" I ask.

He sits on the edge of my bed and says,
"Is there such a thing as bad poetry?"

By his question, I know he writes it.
By mine, he knows I don't want to die.

"And should it rhyme?"
"Rhyme," I say, "can arrive anywhere, anytime—

suddenly, like a stroke, or eventually
like flesh collapsing at the end of the line."

He stands, gestures with a wing,
so I follow him to the hallway's plate glass wall

he says he almost flew through.
We look beyond the sheared lawn

to a graveyard's tilted markers.
Nodding in that direction,

my hospital angel whispers words everyone will hear.

A Better Place

I strike a match to the ginger candle
my candle-crazed friend
from college sent so long ago,

the one whose mother called to say he's gone
to a better place,
that imaginary space like greener grass.

*

A haggard lawn supports us now,
a buffer between mourners and the underworld.
His mother tucks a tissue in her sleeve,

then leads us to her home,
believing things the bereft believe
to keep them strong.

*

Ribbon candy on the piano
recalls the days he played
in the old school ways of sidewalk chalk,

finger paint, and weekly lessons
in this room. Wrong notes,
joy at passages gotten right—

his mother describes
those years with the delight
that memory ignites.

A candle in the hall
burns with our friend's fixation with the night.
We say goodbye. The porch lamp

casts its path along the lawn.
How sudden and complete the dark
when she shuts her door.

In a Small New England Town

I thought it was the fiery maple
outside the hotel window,

but it was your reflection
as you powdered your cheek

with rouge from an organic market
that turned you into a leaf—

a lively leaf, not the kind that falls
but the leaf on a branch

in an impressionist painting,
glowing and indifferent

to the thousands
of viewers who, like me,

stand back, move close,
deciding which part is more

beautiful, walking away from the glass
to give you a kiss on the cheek

that started all this in the first place.

At a Cottage Colony

Someone taps the rim of a pot.
Rice, pasta, polenta, what?

Someone keeps that precious
mess inside and clears the spoon.

The matter's done, a platter served.
Next day at noon, a voice

beyond the privet asks,
"Joe, do you want last night's for lunch?

There's not enough for two."
"No, you have it.

You know you love it more than me,
and I know you."

Bill Knott

(1940–2014)

I'm writing this in purple ink
as was his wont,
a phrase that would have put him
in stitches—another cliché
he'd scorn ungently.
I miss my friend,
whose absence could fill a room
with stories
from those whose lives
he touched and tortured,
like the kid
who quit his class
rather than risk another thesaurus
tossed at his head.
When my son was sick,
Bill wrote
If I believed in god, I'd pray
but since I don't,
here's something to help.
Not cashing the check
made him angry, but stormy
feelings were his domain,
remnants of the orphanage
and army.
He changed the name
of his collected tome
on Amazon every day,
settling for

Dropping Sylvia Plath on Hiroshima
and Other Poems.
An unlikely ladies' man,
lavender ink often leaking down his shirt—
let's leave him
where I saw him last,
on a bed in a Mass Ave. Mattress Firm,
sitting beside a gorgeous novelist,
both of them bouncing
and testing, collapsing
and laughing, then resting.

Possession

When you lose a child,
you learn what you knew all along.

You borrow *Possession* for seven weeks.
You list your boat, *Get Free*, for sale.

You'll never lift that same shirt
from the drawer.

It will always be the one you wore
when you learned

what you knew all along.
Getting through the change

from flesh to bone, heart to soul,
recalls the others still in line.

When you love a child,
you know what you'll lose.

It's unkind of you to stall
and there's a fine for being late.

Possession is past due.

Personal

If anyone knows someone
looking for someone
not yet in the ER

and not recently
off the canvas
after a standing eight,

and if that someone
could care less
if I haven't

done the steps,
learned to read
an Excel actuarial

table
or an X-ray,
please

have them text me
when the sirens
stop

so we can
stay on this carousel
until that second

whirl
called life
after death.

Between *Born Alone* and *Dies Alone* Comes *Lives Alone*

My doctor keeps an eye on all of us
who might skate across a floor
of bathroom steam and not make it to the hall.

A simple phrase appears on every page
of his report—*Lives Alone.*

"You'll Never Walk Alone" is the song
my father named for me when I was born.

He played that record again and again
while indulging his twin passions
of reading maps in a massive atlas
and drinking rye.

You can't fly on one wing, he'd say,
pouring glass after glass.

Now, airplanes and geese glide by my window
on the fifteenth floor.

I'm not strapping on one wing or two.
I'm not trying to fly alongside.
I'm not even walking through a storm alone.

No, I'm here in a chair reading that chart
from my doctor whose office is in the atlas
my father believed contained the world,

a world containing everything not seen on a map.

Making a Will

It was the hour of the costly lawyer
when I dotted i's on a slate-like page.

His office wall displayed a photo
of a lawn where bartenders

drained gin from cocktail shakers
into a festival of glasses

glinting under everyone's chin.
I felt weary debating fractions,

picturing furniture in vans,
and shaking hands with the hand of fate.

A cat, in what looked like the last hour
of his ninth life, rose

from the bottom shelf of torts
and leaned against my leg,

exercising his repertoire
of interrogatives. I understood then,

and I understand now
more than ever,

the questions he kept asking.
I've been asking them myself

at this table
of so many firsts and lasts.

Silk Bouquet

A grammar school girl waits for the bus
on a snow-packed street
where the bus rarely stops.
In one hand, a tote. In the other, a rose.

A petal drops to the icy curb,
and she says, *oh no,*
not in alarm, but mimicking
an adult response.

That single petal settles on the snow
like those at the base of the silk bouquet
my mother plucked and placed
beside the vase to appear they fell.

And, from her desire
to brighten up the world, they did.

Thank you, mortal petal,
for reminding me of my mother's need
to warm our rooms.

It's not just snow that makes us cold.
Time has a climate.

A yellow bus arrives, the door unfolds.

Lew Welch Delivers

It's still here on the rack
at Goodwill, that extra large
button-down black shirt
with a ten percent off
tag for seniors. *Wasabi*
stitched in red on the pocket.
I pick it up for your birthday.
Richard Brautigan was born
this day as well. He, too,
was XL, but not eligible
for the discount when he died.
Besides, it would be hell to ship,
wherever he is. Then again,
maybe Lew Welch delivers.

Frankie the Twister

I'll go it alone, that's how it must be. . . .

After Frankie at the bar finished singing
"I've Gotta Be Me," he blamed
weekends for losing job upon job.

Weekends blamed Mondays.
Mondays, the job.

The job blamed the hours
and the hours, the minutes.

The minutes blamed the seconds.
the seconds, the time clock.
The clock blamed the boss,

and the boss blamed the owner,
James D. O'Reilly
who on Tuesday fired Frankie,
who continues to sing.

Star Market

A hand behind me
taps my arm
to show
two mushrooms
on an open palm.

I allow him
to go ahead
and when he leaves,
the cashier rolls
her eyes and grieves

that in her bones
she feels that soon
she'll meet
a man
with one mushroom.

Two Prose Poems on Water

MALE ADRIFT

Following the dispatcher's report of a "male adrift," the Barnstable police arrived at the Lewis Bay Marina and found Shane Parson flailing near his boat, *The Lily Pad.* After securing the vessel and bringing Parson aboard, police described his speech as slurred. Parson said he was reaching around the motor for a lost bottle opener when he fell into the drink. Police asked him to exit the boat onto a nearby dock where he fell for a second time into the water. The next week, he appeared in court for his fifth offense of driving a boat under the influence and was about to be released on $2,500 bail, provided he remain sober, wear an ankle bracelet gauging his alcohol intake, and not drive a motor vehicle. Parson became agitated at the sentence and began slamming things around, hitting the sergeant-at-arms who rearrested him for battery with a dangerous weapon, to wit: a water pitcher.

WALKING ON WATER

The towels arrived just after you left. I'm sorry you never got to use them. They're from Frontgate and are supposed to be the best, according to Wirecutter, which is owned by the *New York Times*, which I try hard to believe. If I doubt that paper of record at this point in my life, I'm afraid I will falter on my path, just as St. Peter did when Christ told him to walk across the waves. And Peter did, he was heading right toward Christ from his boat! But when a hard wind blew and he looked down at his shoes, he thought, *Oh No! I can't be walking on water!* And so he sank. . . .

If Christ had ordered those towels from Frontgate, the resort towels of long-strand Egyptian cotton, I have a feeling that neither the bath towel nor the hand towel would have arrived in time to dry off St. Peter. So you and I, and Peter and Christ, have at least that much in common.

Roback

Queens, NY

—My father-in-law worked for Bernie Roback, "The Vegetable King of Queens."

—I lived across from Roback's. Your father-in-law always wore a brown suit and fed the pigeons.

—My Uncle Pasquale was Bernie's handicapper for the horses.

—Did Pasquale drive a taxi?

—No, that was Bernie's partner, John.

—Every Halloween we'd fish old fruit from their dumpster to bomb each other and every bus.

—My brother sold Christmas trees there at Christmas time.

—My father-in-law always boosted a wreath when he delivered them to St. Joan's.

—I used to round up shopping carts for Bernie and received a big bag of vegetables in return.

—Your Uncle Pasquale was "a self-employed individual."

—My husband, Joey, drove a cab for John on Sundays.

—Didn't John own a white, '67 Mustang?

—Yes, he bought it on our tenth wedding anniversary. He drove to Bellacicco's bakery on Fridays to pick up paperwork, and then he'd take me to the Cavalier for dinner.

—Your John was handsome.

—Bernie sold Mangiapane bread and it came in a bag picturing Bernie in boxing gloves and the slogan, *The Bread with a Punch.*

—He was a nice man, Bernie. He sat in the back on a crate.

—Always a cigar and a wink!

—I lived next door to him and used to play with his daughter, Peppina.

—My father-in-law always bounced her on his knee.

—I caught Pasquale putting a Snickers in his pocket. He noticed me and said, "Five finger discount!"

—Bernie died young. A heart attack on the Whitestone Bridge going to the Jai-Alai in Connecticut. His car flipped over.

—John maintained there was something fishy about that.

—They were into all kinds of stuff. One time I walked into the rear freezer, and it was filled with fur coats.

—Never got caught though!

—Hooray for them!

—No, they did. I know. My father-in-law snitched on them.

*

Note on "Roback"

from the New York Times

The owner of a Queens produce market
and seven others accused of helping him
steal a million dollars worth of fruit
and vegetables from the Bronx Wholesale Terminal
were arraigned in Queens.
A ninth defendant, a 15-year-old boy,
has been turned over to juvenile court.
Police photographed three of the men
as they unloaded hundreds of cases
of vegetables and fruit from freight cars
at the huge wholesale exchange in the Hunt's Point
section of the Bronx. The produce, stacked
on trucks, was driven to the Roback Open Air Market
in Corona, where police photographed
the defendants unloading the stolen fruits
and vegetables. The president of Roback,
Bernard Roback, 52, was released on $2,000 bail.

Return Home

My mother lit a citrus candle
with no citrus scent,
just the scorched trace of an extinguished moth.

It was the two of us and a stray dog
who pushed its way in,
reminding me of the key I still carried.

She spoke of the dead as if the wind
held the door open
and called everyone out by name.

Some went fast, others lingered,
but the pact they made at birth
had come to an end.

It began to rain as she served tea.
In the middle of the living room
I thought I felt a drop.

Her dementia seemed almost wise,
telling me to burn my boat when I reached the other side.
I held her hand, staring at the notched door

that measured me as a child.
Then I marched through the frame,
the past painted over and erased.

At the Golden Cue

If my father could have put into practice
his insistence that the angle of incidence
equaled the angle of refraction,
he'd have won more games of pool.

He circled the table gracefully,
aiming his cue and lining up invisible margins,
like a surveyor along an expansive lawn.

Sometimes he stretched so far across the rail,
he lifted completely off the ground
except for one toe that trembled
when he pulled back his elbow and followed through.

Scarred oak and worn felt added to the green tableau.

"That's all she wrote," were the only words
the Cue's owner ever spoke.
Susie kept to herself. In a housecoat,
she pushed a broom, then scribbled on the wall
an accounting of the miles she swept.

My father blamed a gleaming light
for a right angle gone wrong
and the loud juke box for missing a routine shot.
If he slipped, he cursed the linoleum's saliva-like sheen.

We buried his cue alongside him
in league with his comical belief that the afterlife
promised chalk cubes forming an igloo-like retreat.

He treasured the notion of a gangs-all-here reunion
full of fun waiting for him,
providing another chance to reignite the rivalries he loved.

He looked forward to that. He used to pat my arm
and say he looked forward to that.

Elegy for My Father

From years at the wheel of tractor-trailers,
he adopted the headlong glare of high beams
facing a runaway truck ramp.

Easy to believe he dated a dancer named "Tabasco"
who sang "It's Been Done Before but Not the Way I Do It."

Hard to know how he lost a knuckle to a penguin
at a diner in Wisconsin.

Harder to explain he discovered poetry
and suggested I visit Gertrude Stein's grave in Paris.

Old age consisted of memories containing lessons.

First-class petty officer, airplane mechanic,
envelope salesman, orderly
in the pediatric ward of Elmhurst General.

His ghost visits me in different guises.

Last night, wearing hospital scrubs,
he said the cries of the infant born blind
were identical to the cries of those who could see.

I see you now, father, when I close my eyes.